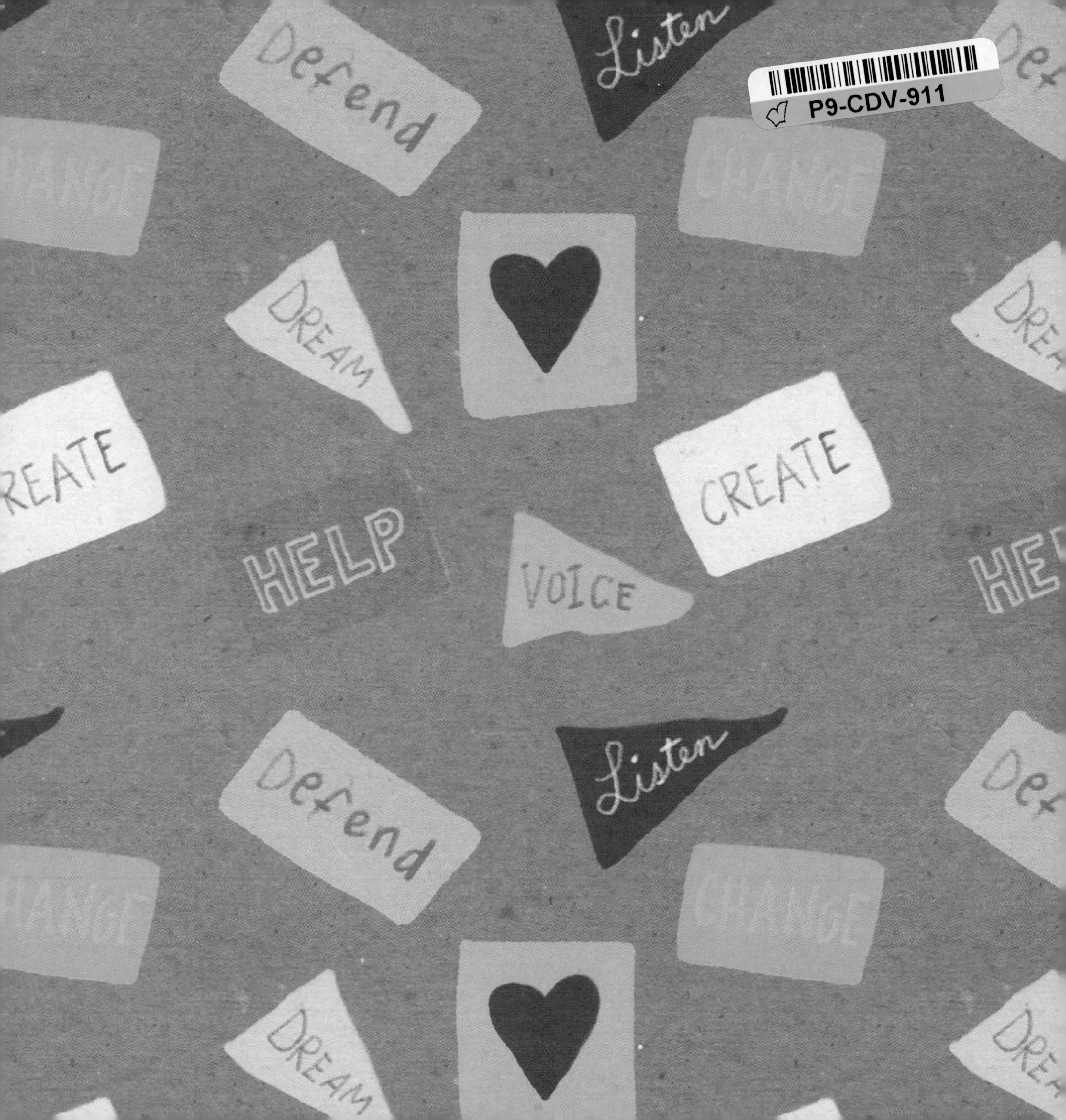
Defend
Listen
CHANGE
DREAM
CREATE
HELP
VOICE

Defend
Listen
Defend
CHANGE
DREAM
DREAM
CREATE
HELP
VOICE
HELP
Defend
Listen
Defend
CHANGE

YOU ARE REVOLUTIONARY

by Cindy Wang Brandt

illustrated by Lynnor Bontigao

beaming books
MINNEAPOLIS

From the moment you were born, you changed the shape of history.
As surely as your heart beat, your existence was revolutionary.

Before you could crawl,
before your first word,
you giggled, you cried,
you declared, "I WILL BE HEARD!"

Now you are bigger,
though you may feel small.
With your eyes wide open
you see the world's not fair for all.

You know deep inside
that every kid has a right
to food, shelter, water,
and a future that's safe and bright.

When you try to ask questions,
speak up about what's unfair,
people tell you to hush,
to wait 'til you're grown to care.

You want to make change
when you see things aren't right.

But you wonder if you're
too little or too shy to fight.

Don't listen to those voices!
There's so much you can do.
You can be part of a revolution,
just by being you.

Listen to your body.
Learn what makes you tick.
What makes your skin feel tingly
and your heart flutter and kick?

If you're a big dreamer
who imagines what others can't see,
you can cast a vision
for how the world should be.

If you experience hardship
and struggle firsthand,
you can share your story.
Raise your voice! Take a stand!

If you're really good at math
and enjoy numbers and counting,
you can help keep track
of problems that are mounting.

HOP
HOP

If you like making jokes
about what's both funny and true,
you can spread joy and humor.
Laughter is revolutionary too.

If you excel at writing words
as mighty as a sword,
you can share a message
in ways that can't be ignored.

If you're a kid who can sing,
play an instrument, or make art,
with your skill and creativity
you can change people's hearts.

If you're always on the move
with energy to spare,
you can knock on doors
and lift signs up in the air.

You can be fierce and feisty,
or you can be soft and tender.
To fix the world's big problems
we need both defenders and menders.

Revolutionaries work together,
side-by-side from the start.
All grown-ups and kids
need to do their part.

Together we'll rise up,
we'll march, and we'll create
a better and fairer world
than what we've seen to date.

HOMES NOT JAILS
WE EXIST
AFFORDABLE HOUSING NOW
END EVICTIONS
EVERYBODY NEEDS A
HOUSING IS A HUMAN RIGHT
HOMES FOR ALL!
2

You'll work hard,
and you'll also have fun!

Every kid is revolutionary—
every last one.

27 26 25 24 23 22 21   1 2 3 4 5 6 7 8

Hardcover ISBN: 978-1-5064-7830-2
eBook ISBN: 978-1-5064-7898-2

Library of Congress Cataloging-in-Publication Data
Names: Brandt, Cindy Wang, 1978- author. | Bontigao, Lynnor, illustrator.
Title: You are revolutionary / by Cindy Wang Brandt ; illustrated by Lynnor
  Bontigao.
Description: Minneapolis, MN : Beaming Books, [2021] | Audience: Ages 5-8.
  | Summary: "This empowering picture book teaches all kids, no matter
  their age or abilities, that they have what it takes to change the
  world. They don't need to wait until they grow up, and they don't even
  need any special skills. They can make a big difference--just as they
  are"-- Provided by publisher.
Identifiers: LCCN 2021001983 (print) | LCCN 2021001984 (ebook) | ISBN
  9781506478302 (hardcover) | ISBN 9781506478982 (ebook)
Subjects: CYAC: Stories in rhyme. | Social action--Fiction.
Classification: LCC PZ8.3.B7353 Yo 2021 (print) | LCC PZ8.3.B7353 (ebook)
  | DDC [E]--dc23
LC record available at https://lccn.loc.gov/2021001983
LC ebook record available at https://lccn.loc.gov/2021001984

VN0004589; 9781506478302; AUG2021

Beaming Books
PO Box 1209
Minneapolis, MN 55440-1209
Beamingbooks.com

TO LIZZY & HAYDEN, FOR
CHANGING MY WORLD.
YOU ARE REVOLUTIONARY.
—CWB

TO MY REVOLUTIONARY
MOM, COL. BONTIGAO.
—LBB

ABOUT THE AUTHOR AND ILLUSTRATOR

CINDY WANG BRANDT is the author of *Parenting Forward: How to Raise Children with Justice, Mercy, and Kindness*. She is the host of the podcast *Parenting Forward* and the Parenting Forward conference. Cindy writes at cindywangbrandt.com. You can also find her on Facebook, Twitter, and Instagram. Cindy lives in Kaohsiung, Taiwan, with her husband and two children.

LYNNOR BONTIGAO has loved drawing ever since she was a young child in the Philippines. Lynnor is also the illustrator of *Jack & Agyu*, written by Justine Villanueva. She is a member of the Society of Children's Book Writers and Illustrators and won the 2020 SCBWI Tomie dePaola Professional Development Award. She lives in New Jersey with her husband, two kids, and one tiny dog.

Listen
Defend
CHANGE
DREAM
CREATE
VOICE
HELP
Listen
Defend
CHANGE
DREAM